AFRICAN AMERICAN ARTISTS & WRITERS

AFRICAN AMERICAN ARTISTS & WRITERS

EDITED BY JOANNE RANDOLPH

Enslow Publishing
101 W. 23rd Street
Suite 240
New York, NY 10011
USA

enslow.com

PIONEERING
AFRICAN
AMERICANS

This edition published in 2018 by
Enslow Publishing, LLC.
101 W. 23rd Street, Suite 240
New York, NY 10011

Additional materials copyright © 2018 by Enslow Publishing, LLC

Library of Congress Cataloging-in-Publication Data

Names: Randolph, Joanne, editor.
Title: African American artists & writers / edited by Joanne Randolph.
Description: New York : Enslow Publishing, 2018. | Series: Pioneering African Americans | Includes bibliographical references and index. | Audience: Grades 5–8.
Identifiers: LCCN 2017021472| ISBN 9780766092518 (library bound) | ISBN 9780766093935 (pbk.) | ISBN 9780766093942 (6 pack)
Subjects: LCSH: African American artists—Biography—Juvenile literature. | African American authors—Biography—Juvenile literature.
Classification: LCC NX512.3.A35 A34 2017 | DDC 700.92/2 [B] —dc23
LC record available at https://lccn.loc.gov/2017021472

Printed in the United States of America

To Our Readers: We have done our best to make sure all website addresses in this book were active and appropriate when we went to press. However, the author and the publisher have no control over and assume no liability for the material available on those websites or on any websites they may link to. Any comments or suggestions can be sent by email to customerservice@enslow.com.

CONTENTS

CHAPTER ONE

WRITING HISTORY 6

CHAPTER TWO

THE HARLEM RENAISSANCE:
A CULTURAL REBIRTH 10

CHAPTER THREE

HARLEM'S PHOTOGRAPHY 22

CHAPTER FOUR

WOMEN WRITERS 33

CHAPTER FIVE

TWO MASTERS WITH THE BRUSH 41

GLOSSARY 46
FURTHER READING 47
INDEX 48

WRITING HISTORY

Despite inequality of access to education, relentless discrimination, and a starkly segregated society, African American artists and writers have made landmark contributions to American art and literature. Works such as *A Raisin in the Son*, *Beloved*, *Their Eyes Were Watching God*, *Invisible Man*, and *I Know Why the Caged Bird Sings* powerfully express the African American experience, expose the injustices of American society, and reveal the hopes, dreams, sorrows, suffering, and enduring achievements of black America.

FROM SLAVERY TO POETRY: PHILLIS WHEATLEY

Phillis Wheatley (1753–1784) was captured in Africa as a young girl and brought to America to be sold as a slave. She would grow up to become America's first published African American poet.

In 1761 John Wheatley and his wife, Susannah, bought the young girl right off the slave ship in Boston Harbor. They named her Phillis. One day the Wheatleys saw Phillis writing on a wall with chalk. Instead of punishing her, they encouraged her to learn to read and write. (This was forbidden to most slaves.)

When she was thirteen, Phillis Wheatley wrote her first poem. It was published in the *Newport Mercury* newspaper in 1767. When she was eighteen, Phillis traveled to England with the Wheatleys' son. There, a friend of the family helped Phillis publish a book of her poetry in 1773. When they returned home, the Wheatleys gave Phillis her freedom. As a free woman, Phillis Wheatley published more poems and an antislavery letter. After meeting George Washington, she wrote a poem for him. When thanking her, General Washington praised her "great poetical talents." Phillis Wheatley is still remembered for her writing and for her journey from slavery to poetry.

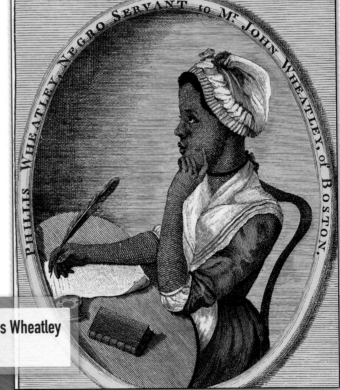

This illustration shows Phillis Wheatley around 1770.

7

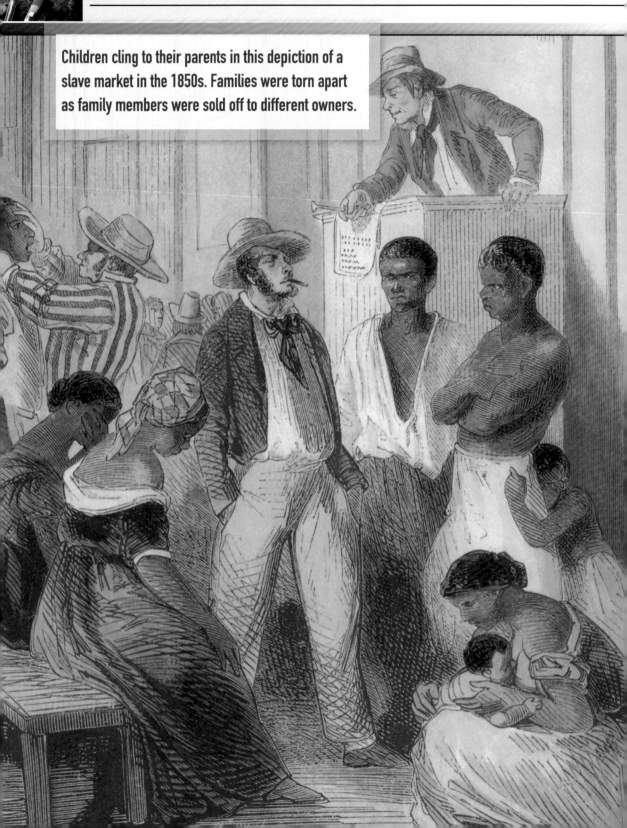

Children cling to their parents in this depiction of a slave market in the 1850s. Families were torn apart as family members were sold off to different owners.

SLAVE GIRL AND AUTHOR: HARRIET JACOBS

Born in North Carolina, Harriet Jacobs (1813–1897) was a slave who hid for seven years in her grandmother's cramped attic, waiting to escape to freedom and be reunited with her children. To pass the time, she read and sewed. Jacobs also corresponded with wealthy white female abolitionists, asking them to help her publish her story.

Jacobs finally escaped to New York, and to her children. Writer and abolitionist Lydia Maria Child agreed to edit Jacobs's manuscript. It was published as *Incidents in the Life of a Slave Girl, Written by Herself* (1861). Although Jacobs changed the names of the main characters, historians have verified that the book is her autobiography and have discovered the identities of her advocates and opponents. When it first came out, it received good reviews, but it quickly fell off the radar when the Civil War broke out. Another century would pass by before interest in the book would be rekindled by a resurgence of attention to minority and women's rights and contributions to society.

CHAPTER TWO

THE HARLEM RENAISSANCE: A CULTURAL REBIRTH

After the Civil War, slavery ended and Reconstruction began. But life did not suddenly become easy for African American people. They would face decades of discrimination and inequality. Many African Americans were looking for ways to improve their lives. Great waves of African Americans migrated to northern cities to take advantage of the many factory jobs that opened up in response to World War I (1914–1918). Unfortunately, social attitudes of the early twentieth century forced them to settle in segregated urban housing. So, they created bustling black metropolises—cities within cities. This caused a period of remarkable artistic and intellectual activity in New York City's African American community, leading to the Harlem Renaissance.

SPREADING THE MESSAGE THROUGH THE ARTS

While other cities saw similar developments and had their own rebirths, at the time, New York City was very much the cultural

A 1932 movie poster for *Harlem Is Heaven* illustrates Harlem's thriving culture, which attracted many authors, artists, musicians, actors, and more to live there.

capital of the United States. It was a publishing and writing center, home to most of the significant museums and galleries, and site of major music venues. Thus, the largely African American neighborhood called Harlem, located in northern Manhattan, is viewed as the starting point of the modern black artistic movement. From around 1923 to the beginning of the Great Depression in 1929, black writers and artists who gathered in Harlem generated an extraordinary amount and diversity of conversation, debate, and culture.

An important first impact of the Harlem Renaissance was the wide range of political action taken by both organizations and individuals who demanded improvements in African American economic and educational opportunities. After black soldiers had participated honorably during World War I, they hoped to come back to an America ready to accept and recognize their contributions and accomplishments. But outbreaks of racial violence due to the legality of Jim Crow laws often dashed these hopes.

A number of individuals, including W. E. B. Du Bois, James Weldon Johnson, and Arthur Schomburg, began to reflect on how cultural activity might aid the African American community in its struggle to better its situation. In the pages of *The Crisis*, the magazine of the National Association for the Advancement of Colored People (NAACP), Du Bois and novelist Jessie Fauset encouraged conversation about how creativity in the arts might contribute to a better understanding of and respect for the African American experience.

The poet Langston Hughes made an important point in this debate with his essay "The Negro Artist and the Racial Mountain," which was published in 1926 in the magazine *The Nation*. Hughes endorsed the idea that the arts could have a positive role to play in the betterment of the black community. He insisted, however, that the

W. E. B. Du Bois was a leader in the civil rights movement, working tirelessly to obtain equal rights and treatment for African Americans.

work produced must embrace the whole African American culture and not merely mimic white standards, styles, and expectations. "We younger Negro artists who create now intend to express our individual dark-skinned selves without fear or shame," wrote Hughes.

Young African American writers took up Hughes's challenge. Zora Neale Hurston, Wallace Thurman, Jean Toomer, and Nella Larsen all made enormous contributions. The Harlem Renaissance included more than the emergence of strong black literary voices. Painting, sculpture, music, theater, and dance were affected, too. Painter Aaron Douglas, actor Paul Robeson, dancer Florence Mills, bandleader Duke Ellington, sculptor Richmond Barthe, playwright Willis Richardson, and composer R. Nathaniel Dett were products of, as well as contributors to, the fabric and depth of the movement.

Most historians and critics suggest that the Harlem Renaissance had run its course by the mid-1930s. The onset of the Great

Zora Neale Hurston was an author and anthropologist who wrote about what it was like to be black in America.

Depression and its economic difficulties ate away at much of the philanthropy and other support that had allowed black artists to experiment with their crafts. Some historians argue that the movement continued more energetically in other cities, especially Chicago, Illinois. Others worry that the emphasis on a celebration of black cultural achievements overlooks the difficult living conditions of most African Americans in urban settings.

There is general agreement, however, that the Harlem Renaissance is crucial to the understanding of all twentieth-century American art and culture. While Hughes's challenge was directed specifically to African Americans, the struggle to be a full, satisfied individual appeals to all people, regardless of their background and roots.

YOUNG LANGSTON

James Mercer Langston Hughes was born in Joplin, Missouri, on February 1, 1902, to Carrie Mercer Langston and James Nathaniel

Hughes. Carrie Langston, a thoughtful woman and dedicated mother, had literary interests herself. James Hughes was an extremely ambitious man despite numerous frustrations. Denied an opportunity to take the Oklahoma bar exam in order to become a lawyer, and disappointed because of continued discrimination in Missouri, James decided to seek his fortune in Mexico. Following his father's departure in 1903, Langston led a rather unsettled childhood. He

Langston Hughes, pictured here in 1959, was an influential writer and leader of the Harlem Renaissance.

spent much of it living with his grandmother in Lawrence, Kansas. For brief periods of time, Topeka, Kansas, and Colorado Springs, Colorado, were also home.

During all this moving around, Langston's mother encouraged his interest in reading. His grandmother, Mary Leary, was the widow of one of John Brown's famous raiders at Harpers Ferry. Keenly interested in local and regional politics, she once took Langston to hear the famed African American political and educational leader Booker T. Washington. Family friends Uncle and Auntie Reed exposed him to the vibrancy of African American religious traditions.

As a teenager, Langston had to contend with more family moves. In 1914 he was taken first to Lincoln, Illinois, where his mother remarried. Later, he moved to Cleveland, Ohio, where he was lucky enough to remain for all four years of high school. He began to take an active interest in politics and looked for opportunities to hear the most important speakers and lecturers of the day. A teacher, Ethel Weimer, introduced him to the work of the "Chicago School" of poetry, especially that of Vachel Lindsay and Carl Sandburg. These new poets were known for their interest in the lives of common people, presenting human dilemmas in recognizable, everyday speech rather than elevated and highly structured verse.

High school summers provided the opportunity for travel, which eventually became one of Hughes's most important interests and commitments.

Around 1918 he began to visit his father on his ranch in Mexico. While the trips allowed the young Langston to see a great deal of North America and its people, they also generated real tensions. Although unsure about what to do with his life, Langston knew he did not share his father's ambition that he become a professional engineer. On one of his journeys, he took a scrap of paper, not long after he crossed the Mississippi River, and penned one of his most famous poems, "The Negro Speaks of Rivers." It was not long after this that Langston decided to move to New York City.

HARLEM POET

It was a September morning in 1921. Nineteen-year-old Hughes stood on the corner of Lenox Avenue feeling good. But being there felt a little crazy, too, as if he had finally come home, though he had never been to Harlem before.

With a week to go before beginning classes at Columbia University, he got a room at the YMCA. That afternoon, he crossed the street to visit the Harlem Branch Library, where the librarians made him feel right at home.

He spent the next few days mapping Harlem with his feet. The great dark expanse of this island within an island fascinated him. In 1921 Harlem ran from 125th Street north to 145th and from Madison Avenue to Eighth Avenue. Eighty thousand African Americans were packed into the long rows of tenements as the flood of southern blacks continued to roll north.

Hughes had begun to write poetry in high school in Cleveland. One of his teachers had encouraged him to find his own lyric voice, and the school paper published some of his work.

But Hughes found Columbia too big and too cold and the instructors too busy to bother with a black student who needed help. However, he kept writing poems and sent several to *The Crisis*. It published one, which began, "I am a Negro/Black as the night is

This street scene shows businesses along 125th Street near Eighth Avenue in Harlem in the 1920s. The street likely looked similar when Langston Hughes first arrived.

black/Black as the depths of my Africa." The readers liked the poem so much that *The Crisis* published more.

College did not seem right for Hughes, and he left after one year. After a year of working and writing poetry in New York, he found a job as a steward on a freighter bound for Africa. He was twenty-one and on his own. As the ship made stops at ports along the western shore of Africa, he saw that blacks lived under white laws made abroad for the black colonies, laws that were enforced by whip and gun.

His next job on a freighter brought him to France. He left the ship to discover the Paris every young poet dreamed about. He worked in nightclubs as a doorman, dishwasher, and cook. Alone in his tiny room, he continued to write poetry, fitting the rhythms of jazz into the rhythm of words, and sent his poems off to New York. A magazine bought three of them for $24.50—the first time he had ever been paid for writing. When he lost his job in Paris, he worked his way home on an American ship.

Back in Harlem, Hughes found himself among several black writers and artists and began friendships that would endure. But he was penniless and could not find work. In early 1925, he moved to Washington, DC, taking jobs in a laundry, as a clerk, and then as a bellboy in a hotel. His big break came when the popular white poet Vachel Lindsay read Hughes's poems to a large audience, praising them highly. Overnight, newspapers across the country spread the story of this new poet.

It was the beginning of Hughes's fame but not his fortune. He won literary prizes, was published in many places, and found his way back to Harlem in 1925. There Carl Van Vechten, a widely known white writer who befriended many black artists, took Hughes's poems to a publisher, suggesting that they would make a good book. When Hughes's book *The Weary Blues* appeared in 1926, critics hailed it as powerful, warm, and lyrical.

Still, Hughes felt that his education was unfinished. He wanted to go back to college "in order to be of more use to my race and America," he said. The oldest black school in the country, Lincoln University in Pennsylvania, admitted him. But how could he afford to go without a dime in his pocket? Amy Spingarn, a white woman who admired his poetry, offered to pay his way through Lincoln.

He spent summers in New York, working and immersing himself in Harlem life. All his artist friends were trying to find their roots and new ways to shape black life into art. Hughes experimented with forms derived from black culture. He voiced the spirit of the blues, of spirituals, folk ballads, and gospel songs. His pioneering use of blues forms and jazz rhythms would be the major innovation in the poetry of the Harlem Renaissance.

A second book of his poems came out in 1927. And soon after graduation from Lincoln, his novel *Not Without Laughter* appeared in 1930. Through its characters, he explored the challenges young blacks had to face in a racist society.

In 1929 the Great Depression hit the United States. Even with millions of people jobless and homeless, Hughes decided to try to make a living solely by writing. He made ends meet by traveling the country in an old car and giving readings of his poems at black schools, colleges, and churches. This was the first chance for cotton pickers and college students to see and hear an African American poet.

Hughes's travels would take him across this country and around the world. He wrote articles, poems, and stories based on his wanderings. He founded a theater in Harlem and wrote plays for it. He

In this 1964 photograph, Langston Hughes interviews a panel in a television segment about the Harlem community and its residents.

wrote a movie script, his autobiography, and stories about Jesse B. Semple, a Harlem character he had met in a bar. Hughes often worked with composers, writing the story and lyrics for operas, musical folk comedies, and gospel shows. He wrote many books for young readers on black heroes, musicians, jazz, the West Indies, and Africa. He took part in many festivals of music, poetry, and the arts both at home and abroad.

Hughes's life sounds as though it was great fun, and in truth it was. But it was also a life of hardship and many disappointments. Throughout it, he suffered from the discrimination and segregation so common among African Americans and was hounded because of his political views. None of his writings earned him great financial reward, but he lived generously, devoted to helping anyone whom he could. He died in 1967 at the age of sixty-five.

CHAPTER THREE

HARLEM'S PHOTOGRAPHY

African American identity had long been framed by the viewpoints of white Americans, leaving African Americans feeling inferior and out of place. The Harlem Renaissance changed that to some degree. African American artists and photographers looked with their own eyes at the vibrant culture and brilliant black minds all around them and decided to frame a new picture.

PHOTOGRAPHING THE AFRICAN AMERICAN ELITE

James Latimer Allen (1907–1977) was born and raised in New York City. He came of age at the beginning of the Harlem Renaissance. While attending DeWitt Clinton High School, Allen discovered photography and developed his artistic aspirations. Many of Allen's contemporaries, including Countee Cullen, Charles Alston, and Richard Bruce Nugent, also attended this school and went on to become prominent members of the Renaissance. While still in school,

Many Harlem photographers strove to capture images that showed what life in Harlem was like. James Latimer Allen took this photo of children sculpting soap models in a Harlem art workshop.

Allen apprenticed at a lithography firm, where he further developed his skills and imagined pursuing a career as an artist-photographer.

By 1926 Allen was ready to launch his career as a portrait photographer. The writer Wallace Thurman gave Allen his first opportunity to exhibit his photographs in a show at an apartment building at 267 West 136th Street. Many of the Renaissance artists and writers, including Langston Hughes and Zora Neale Hurston, lived there. Allen's work soon appeared in the prestigious Harmon Foundation exhibits, which were the major showcases for black

This is one of the portraits that Allen took of Langston Hughes as a young man.

artists and other important exhibitions of the period. African American journals such as *Opportunity, The Messenger,* and *The Crisis* reproduced Allen's images frequently.

Allen ran a successful portrait photography studio at 213 West 121st Street. His clients were a who's who of Harlem's leading figures, including Countee Cullen, W. E. B. Du Bois, James Weldon Johnson, Nella Larsen, and A'Lelia Walker. Allen's patrons desired photographs that embodied the same positive outlook they had about themselves, and they appreciated the sophisticated, modern look that he achieved.

During World War II, Allen entered military service and closed his studio, never resuming his career as a photographer. His body of work is remembered and celebrated because it provides a vision of the artists, writers, and intellectuals who shaped this important period in African American history and how they wanted to be remembered.

PHOTOS BY GUARANTEE

Even before James Allen came on the scene in Harlem, James VanDerZee (1886–1983) had been focusing his lens on the people of Harlem and capturing life with his own unique style. James VanDerZee's ability to record the dignity of black life in Harlem through his camera lens made him a prominent figure in the African American community.

Influential Harlem photographer James VanDerZee is pictured here in 1977.

25

VanDerZee left Virginia for the East Coast in 1908. After several moves and a separation from his wife, Kate, he and his friend Gaynella Greenlee opened Guarantee Photo Studio in 1917 in Harlem. The two divided the responsibilities between them: Greenlee managed the studio and VanDerZee took the portraits. Families, church groups, social clubs, lodges, and athletic leagues all clamored to have their photographs taken at Guarantee by Harlem's best photographer.

Meanwhile, Greenlee's husband had died and Kate had agreed to a divorce. VanDerZee and Greenlee were married.

Not long after Guarantee Photo Studio opened, the United States entered World War I. Young black soldiers represented the best and brightest of Harlem, and they often flocked to Guarantee to pose gallantly in their uniforms. The war ended in November 1918, and, on February 17, 1919, VanDerZee stood ready with his camera as thousands of people waited along Fifth Avenue to cheer the black soldiers of the 369th Regiment, who were returning home to Harlem after the war.

VanDerZee's popularity increased throughout the Harlem Renaissance. For example, VanDerZee served as the official photographer for Black Nationalist leader Marcus Garvey and his Universal Negro Improvement Association (UNIA), helping promote the UNIA's message of "Africa for the Africans." In addition, some of the more notable individuals of the Renaissance movement, such as Du Bois, Cullen, Van Vechten, and Hurston, all requested VanDerZee to take their pictures.

Despite VanDerZee's celebrity status in Harlem, he and Greenlee told all their customers that Guarantee was readily accessible to everyone in the community. They also made it clear that they

In this portrait, VanDerZee has captured an elaborately dressed dancer in 1925, highlighting the beauty and vibrance of Harlem culture through his subject.

VanDerZee photographs a group of African American members of the Zionist Temple in 1929 in front of the building, highlighting the diversity within Harlem.

welcomed walk-in customers. Once inside VanDerZee's studio, every client received special attention.

In 1928 VanDerZee had to change the name of his studio after an attorney informed him that "the name Guarantee was reserved for banks and trust companies." As the new name, VanDerZee chose G.G.G. Photo Studio, in honor of his wife, Gaynella Greenlee.

Then the Great Depression arrived. VanDerZee's studio, however, was still drawing many patrons. Photos from this time show simple and elaborate picture frames adorning the countertops and walls.

VanDerZee and Greenlee managed to adapt and accommodate to the economic and social changes in Harlem throughout the 1940s and 1950s. But by the 1960s, VanDerZee and Greenlee were living in virtual poverty. People's tastes in photographs were changing. Many preferred informal snapshots to posed studio pictures. Technology was also changing. Cameras were easier to use, and more people were opting to take their own shots.

However, in 1969, New York's Metropolitan Museum of Art hosted an exhibition titled "Harlem on My Mind," which showcased life during the Harlem Renaissance in a variety of media. It included VanDerZee's work and highlighted his documentation, through photographs, of Harlem's glory days. By the 1970s, VanDerZee had garnered a new audience, introducing them to the magic that had been made at Guarantee Photo Studio and at G.G.G. Photo Studio.

FELLOW PHOTOGRAPHERS

Through his camera's lens, James VanDerZee recorded the spirit and people of Harlem for more than fifty years. His photographs document the daily happenings associated with Harlem's emerging black middle class, as well as special occasions such as birthdays, weddings, baptisms, and recitals. In addition to capturing images of the local community, this New England native also captured on film the political and religious activities that occurred throughout Harlem. However, it is important to know that VanDerZee was not the first, nor the last, black photographer to have African Americans as subjects or to own a studio.

CORNELIUS MARION BATTEY

Cornelius Marion Battey, better known as C. M. Battey was born in 1873 in Augusta, Georgia, Battey spent much of his time traveling, especially to Cleveland, Ohio, and New York City. His most significant work, however, was done while he was director of the photography department he established at Tuskegee Institute (now Tuskegee University) in Tuskegee, Alabama. Battey primarily photographed students; faculty, including the founder of the college, Booker T. Washington; and social and academic activities. Battey's images offered a unique and informative view of college life at one of the country's major Historically Black Colleges and Universities (HBCUs).

C. M. Battey took this photograph of Booker T. Washington.

Marvin and Morgan Smith, pictured here in 1982, used their work to help change stereotypes and to improve the image of African American people in the United States. They wanted to show outsiders that the Harlem community was home to hard-working, decent people.

MORGAN SMITH AND MARVIN SMITH

Like VanDerZee, most black photographers at the time sought to counter negative stereotypes and depicted their subjects with great dignity and grace. Among those who were masters of this style were the twin brothers Morgan (1910–1993) and Marvin Smith (1910–2003). Born to sharecroppers in Nicholasville, Kentucky, the two traveled to Harlem in 1933 to pursue a career in the arts. As talented artists, the Smith brothers not only focused on photography but also perfected their painting skills and kept abreast of all technological advances. As a result, from the 1930s into the 1950s, they had an active studio business and, at the same time, found work in television and in photojournalism.

In addition to depicting the lives of Harlem's residents, the twins' photos documented the social and political history of Harlem as well. The Smiths took pictures of daily events that could easily have been forgotten, such as the community's first black fireman and first female juror.

ELISE FORREST HARLESTON

Another 1930s photographer was Elise Forrest Harleston (1891–1970). A former student of Battey's when both were at Tuskegee, she owned her own studio in Charleston, South Carolina. One of the few female photographers at the time, Harleston combined two media—photography and painting—in her portraits. Harleston primarily photographed the elders of Charleston accompanied by or also represented in a painting created by her husband.

Over the years, interest in learning more about VanDerZee and his contemporaries has continually increased. As a result, it seems certain that in discussions about American photography, talented African American photographers will be recognized for their significant contributions.

CHAPTER FOUR

WOMEN WRITERS

In addition to all the works of African American male authors and artists, there was also a growing body of works by African American women. These women were exploring their cultural identities, not only from the perspective of their struggle with race, but also with the inequities they faced as women.

A RAISIN IN THE SUN

On March 11, 1959, the first play by a black woman to be produced on Broadway opened. Its title was *A Raisin in the Sun*; its author, a young playwright named Lorraine Hansberry.

The play struck a chord in the heart of almost everyone who saw it. Although it was a play about an African American family, the issues it presents transcend race. *A Raisin in the Sun* went on to win the New York Drama Critics Circle Award as the best American play of 1959. Two years later, the play was turned into a film, and then, in 1974, into a musical titled *Raisin*, which won the Tony Award for the best musical that year. The name of the play comes from a line in the poem "Harlem" by Langston Hughes.

Lorraine Hansberry wrote other plays and screenplays in addition to *A Raisin in the Sun*, but they did not meet with as much success.

Lorraine Hansberry (1930–1965) was twenty-eight years old when *A Raisin in the Sun* opened on Broadway. It was her first play. She wrote it in response to being disgusted by the whole body of material being written by African Americans.

The playwright grew up in Chicago. Her father was a banker and real estate broker, and the family prospered. Her uncle was an African American scholar at Howard University, and the entire family was involved in civil rights. When she was young, Lorraine Hansberry met many famous men and women of the time in her parents' living room, including Paul Robeson, Duke Ellington, and Olympic gold medalist Jesse Owens.

A Raisin in the Sun has been translated into thirty different languages and is still produced on stages around the country each year. Sadly, while her second play, *The Sign in Sidney Brustein's Window*, was being produced on Broadway, the playwright was stricken with cancer, and she died at the age of thirty-four.

THE CAGED BIRD SINGS

Maya Angelou (1928–2014) is celebrated as one of the most notable contemporary American novelists. She was also a poet, actor, songwriter, journalist, playwright, historian, singer, civil rights activist, and producer. Angelou is perhaps best known for her 1969 book *I Know Why the Caged Bird Sings*. The first of five autobiographical works, it became an instant bestseller and was nominated for the National Book Award. Critics argue that although her book speaks specifically about Angelou's own tumultuous experiences as a black woman growing up in the United States, its theme of personal

Maya Angelou was a prolific and successful writer who began her career as a dancer and singer. She was a leader in the civil rights movement as well.

strength and triumph over challenges is one with which people around the world can identify.

I Know Why the Caged Bird Sings is a coming-of-age story that speaks not only to the harsh realities of growing up as a black child in a segregated society, but also to the search for an identity in the face of personal struggle. Angelou vividly describes her feelings of abandonment when her mother sends her and her older brother to live with their grandmother in Stamps, Arkansas. She learns to grow up quickly since life in rural sharecropping communities during the Great Depression was often difficult.

In her completely segregated world, Angelou witnesses how racism, sexism, and black powerlessness negatively impact both her life and the lives of other black people. As a result, she develops a deep hatred for her own skin, which she feels is responsible for keeping her locked in an "ugly black dream."

Angelou writes that when she is seven years old, she is raped by her mother's boyfriend. Because the guilt and shame she feels is overwhelming, she slips into isolation and becomes mute for five years. To overcome the deeply painful emotions, she finds comfort in reading, and uses books to escape. Her grandmother, whom she calls Momma, serves as a symbol of strength and quiet dignity in her life. Momma teaches Angelou that she has no choice but to fight her way through the difficulties and injustices she will encounter. Gradually, through the love and support of others, Angelou begins to speak again. By drawing on the strength of Momma and the other women around her, Angelou is able to find her own courage and push beyond the feelings of inadequacy and inferiority to find her true self. Only then is she able to hear the song of strength and power in her own voice.

Toni Morrison has won countless awards for her writing, including the Nobel Prize for Literature.

NOBEL FOR MORRISON

For many years, African American women writers had struggled to argue that their experience and concerns were central and unavoidable in American life. Too often, they were dismissed for being narrow in their outlook.

This view changed in 1993 when the Swedish Academy announcing Toni Morrison as the winner of the Nobel Prize wrote that "the most enduring impression [Morrison's novels] leave is of empathy, compassion with one's fellow human beings." Finally, the message had been received that these stories were not outside the cultural heritage of the United States but in fact central to its richness and complexity.

Toni Morrison was born Chloe Anthony Wofford on February 18, 1931. She grew up in Lorain, Ohio, a small industrial city with a closely-knit black community that often felt very much under siege from both racism and economic hardship, despite the fact that it was located in the North. Morrison learned to value the ways in which local people managed under difficult conditions, and she followed closely the role storytelling played as a means of educating and recording informal history.

Morrison has written several novels, a play, and numerous books for children co-written with her son Slade Morrison. The novels deal, in a sophisticated way, with the challenges that ordinary and sometimes extraordinary Americans face as they seek love and justice in the world.

Sometimes, Morrison draws upon the stock of stories she learned in Ohio in order to dramatize her tales of loss and confusion. In other works, she looked to African American history or folklore for source material, and even to classical mythology and the Bible. Morrison wants her readers to connect with the characters and to care about them but, at the same time, to resist the temptation to simplify their existence.

For younger readers, Morrison's novel *Song of Solomon* (1977) is a good introduction to her style because it relies on familiar stories that many already know—for example, the Greek poet Homer's tale of Ulysses, parables from the New Testament, and family sagas and poetry from the Old Testament.

Over the course of her writing career, Morrison has become ever more interested in the emotional legacy of slavery. She wonders about the ways in which people are all haunted by this tragic portion of American history and what it will take for real reconciliation to happen. In her novel *Beloved* (1987), she gives life to these feelings in the form of one of her characters, the ghost of a child whose mother chose to kill her rather than have her live life as a slave. It is a terrifying story that makes readers struggle with the awful choices African American women must have faced knowing that most slave owners did not care about slave families.

Her later novels—*Jazz* (1992), *Paradise* (1998), and *Love* (2003)—have all focused on acts of violence that prevent meaningful connections between people from ever taking hold. These more recent works are no easier to read than her first novel, *The Bluest Eye* (1969). Morrison's readers must be patient and be open to changing the way in which they see the world, recognizing the horror as well as the beauty of it.

CHAPTER FIVE

TWO MASTERS WITH THE BRUSH

olk art is sometimes defined as art that comes from the "common" people, or the folk. During the 1930s and 1940s, folk art became rather popular in the United States. Critics and collectors called their creators "primitive" artists, largely because they rarely followed the guidelines of formal art. The shapes, textures, and colors common to Africa are detected in pieces by some black folk artists. More specifically, the spirit of black America is reflected in the work of painters such as Clementine Hunter and Horace Pippin.

CLEMENTINE HUNTER

Clementine Hunter was a folk artist who recorded her people's history in "memory paintings." She was born on Hidden Hill Plantation in Louisiana around Christmastime in 1886. When she was young, her family moved to the Cane River region of Louisiana, where the people in the community spoke mainly French. Eventually her family settled at Melrose Plantation, where

This is Clementine Hunter's painting *Picking Cotton*. She depicted the daily life of her community in her simple, colorful paintings.

Hunter began working in the cotton fields. In 1924 she married Emmanuel Hunter, who taught her how to speak English. Later, Hunter was moved to the "big house," where she served as a cook for the Henry family, who owned Melrose.

In the 1930s, many visiting artists came to Melrose Plantation. Cammie Henry, the family matriarch, wanted to preserve the community's art. Hunter recalls that she began painting after she was instructed to clean up and throw away the unused paints left by a Melrose guest. Instead, she took the half-empty jars back to her cabin, where she made her own pictures.

Hunter depicted what she knew best—African Americans who picked cotton, cut sugar cane, and gathered figs and harvested pecans, as well as those who celebrated life through baptisms, weddings, dances, and church affairs around Cane River. She painted her community on window shades, wine jugs, snuff bottles, cutting boards, water bottles, gourds, iron skillets, and canvases.

The money Hunter began earning in the early 1940s helped to support her art. When her husband became ill, she held an exhibit that allowed visitors to see her work for twenty-five cents. In 1945 she received the prestigious Rosenwald Fund Fellowship. She also became the first African American to have her paintings displayed at the Delgado Museum (now the New Orleans Museum of Art). Hunter, however, had to sneak into the exhibit because she was not allowed to view her paintings at the same time as whites.

Hunter touched people's lives through art. She was in her late sixties when she finished a mural at Melrose. In her late seventies, Hunter experimented with abstract painting, but returned to distinct images of her community. Her work was soon being exhibited in New York and California. In 1976 Hunter's art was featured in the United Nations' UNICEF calendar. Ten years later, Hunter received an honorary doctorate of fine arts from Northwestern State University of Louisiana.

When Hunter died on January 1, 1988, at age 101, she left as her legacy thousands of paintings that captured the beauty of her people.

This 1943 painting by Horace Pippin is called *Sunday Morning Breakfast*. Like Hunter's work, Pippin's art captured everyday scenes from African American life.

HORACE PIPPIN

Horace Pippin is possibly the most famous African American folk painter of his time. Born into poverty in West Chester, Pennsylvania, in 1888, Pippin spent part of his life in Goshen, New York. At around age fourteen, he left school and began doing odd jobs to support his mother. Pippin worked as a peddler, warehouseman, and even a porter. Then, in 1917, he enlisted in the US Army. He was a member of the 369th Colored Infantry Regiment, the first black regiment to fight overseas for the United States in World War I. Known for their bravery, members of the 369th were dubbed the "Hell Fighters" by French allies. As a result of a sniper's shot in the right shoulder, Pippin lost the use of his right hand.

In spite of the serious injury, Pippin began painting in 1928. Pippin used his World War I experiences to create his paintings. It took the untrained artist three years to complete his first known oil painting, *End of War: Starting Home*.

Pippin's paintings also depict landscapes, African American life, and religious themes. He used bright, rich colors to make his flat forms. His stories are clear, rather than abstract. Pippin was uninterested when one of his supporters tried to encourage him to study impressionist painters, who used very little detail.

Included in Pippin's collection of 150 oil drawings and wood panels are *The Whipping*, *Giving Thanks*, and *Harmonizing*. Pippin was also honored for such paintings as *John Brown Going to His Hanging*, based on the 1859 execution of the white abolitionist. Pippin received a prize for this painting from the Pennsylvania Academy of Fine Arts.

In 1938 Pippin became the first black artist to have his work shown at the Museum of Modern Art in New York City. The exhibit was called Masters of Popular Painting. Before his death in 1946, Pippin continued to make powerful statements about freedom and justice through his paintings on war and peace.

GLOSSARY

abstract art Art that depicts its subject material conceptually rather than realistically.

autobiography The written history of oneself authored by oneself.

Black Nationalist An advocate of the social and political movement that calls for African Americans to separate themselves culturally, politically, and economically from the white community.

Great Depression The period of severe economic downturn that began in 1929 and lasted through most of the 1930s.

Jim Crow laws The legal practice of discriminating against and suppressing African Americans.

lithography A printing process in which the image is rendered on a flat stone surface and treated to retain ink while the non-image areas are treated to repel ink.

matriarch The female head of a large, extended family.

metropolis A major city of a region that is regarded as a center of specific activities.

philanthropy The effort to increase the well-being of humankind, as through charitable aid.

photojournalism A type of news reporting that tells a story through pictures.

porter A railroad employee who waits on passengers in sleeping or parlor cars.

Renaissance A revival period of intellectual or artistic achievement and vigor.

sharecropper A tenant farmer who works land for a share of the produce.

BOOKS

Antal, Lara. *James Van Der Zee*. New York, NY: Cavendish Square Publishing, 2016.

Bernier, Celeste-Marie. *Suffering and Sunset: World War I in the Art and Life of Horace Pippin*. Philadelphia, PA: Temple University Press, 2015.

Borus, Audrey. *Reading and Interpreting the Works of Maya Angelou*. New York, NY: Enslow Publishing, 2017.

Crayton, Lisa A. *Reading and Interpreting the Works of Toni Morrison*. New York, NY: Enslow Publishing, 2016.

Rohan, Rebecca. *Langston Hughes*. New York, NY: Cavendish Square Publishing, 2016.

WEBSITES

Digital Schomburg Collection of African American Women Writers of the 19th Century
digital.nypl.org/schomburg/writers_aa19/toc.html
Discover the works and biographies of Phillis Wheatley, Harriet Jacobs, and other women writers.

PBS, The Harlem Renaissance
www.pbs.org/wnet/jimcrow/stories_events_harlem.html
Learn more about the important cultural movement and follow links to other pages that focus on different aspects of African American history.

Academy of American Poets, Langston Hughes
www.poets.org/poetsorg/poet/langston-hughes
Read a biography of Langston Hughes as well as his works.

INDEX

A
Allen, James Latimer, 22–23
Alston, Charles, 22
Angelou, Maya, 35–37, 47

B
Battey, Cornelius Marion, 30, 32

C
Cullen, Countee, 22, 24

D
DuBois, W. E. B., 12, 13, 24, 26
Duke Ellington, 13, 35

G
Garvey, Marcus, 26
Greenlee, Gaynella, 26, 28, 29

H
Hansberry, Lorraine, 33–35
Henry, Cammie, 42
Hughes, Langston, 12–13,
    14–21, 23–24, 33, 47
Hunter, Clementine, 41, 42
Hurston, Zora Neale, 13–14, 23

J
Jacobs, Harriet, 9, 47

Johnson, James Weldon, 12

M
Morrison, Toni, 38–40, 47

P
Pippin, Horace, 41, 44, 45, 47

R
Robeson, Paul, 13, 35

S
Smith, Marvin, 31
Smith, Morgan, 31

T
Thurman, Wallace, 13

V
VanDerZee, James, 25–29,
    31–32, 47

W
Walker, A'Lelia, 24
Washington, Booker T., 30
Wheatley, John, 7
Wheatley, Phillis, 6–7, 47